NATIVE NATIONS OF NORTH AMERICA

Life of the California Coast Nations

Molly Aloian & Bobbie Kalman

Crabtree Publishing Company

www.crabtreebooks.com

Life of the California Coast Nations

Created by Bobbie Kalman

Dedicated by the Editorial team
For two tiny treasures, Emma Nesbitt and Jane Miller

Editor-in-Chief
Bobbie Kalman

Writing team
Molly Aloian
Bobbie Kalman

Substantive editors
Amanda Bishop
Deanna Brady

Editors
Kristina Lundblad
Kelley MacAulay
Kathryn Smithyman

Art director
Robert MacGregor

Design
Katherine Berti

Production coordinator
Katherine Berti

Photo research
Crystal Sikkens

Consultant
Terry L. Jones, Associate Professor of Anthropology, California Polytechnic State University, San Luis Obispo

Photographs and reproductions
© Bryn Barnard: page 5
Inga Spence/Index Stock: page 31
W. Langdon Kihn/National Geographic Society Image Collection: pages 6, 28
Nativestock.com: pages 7, 12, 23
© N.Carter/North Wind Picture Archives: page 29
© North Wind Picture Archives: pages 26, 27
Painting, *Chumash Ways*, by Mitchell E. Robles, www.mitchrobles.com: page 30
Ann Thiermann, California muralist & illustrator, www.annthiermann.com :
    pages 8, 9, 10-11, 14, 18 (top), 19 (bottom), 21, 24
© Michael K. Ward: front cover, title page (except background), pages 16, 17 (top)
Other images by Digital Stock

Illustrations
Barbara Bedell: pages 12 (top), 13 (necklace), 15 (top), 17 (log raft), 18 (bottom),
    19 (top), 22, 23, 25 (steatite objects, seed beater, and basket)
Katherine Berti: border, pages 4 (map of California coast), 12 (middle and
    bottom), 13 (deer), 15 (middle and bottom), 17 (balsa), 20 (acorns)
Margaret Amy Salter: back cover (hide background), title page (background),
    pages 4 (crab and clams), 7, 13 (background), 25 (all except steatite objects,
    seed beater, and basket), 31
Bonna Rouse: back cover (village), pages 4 (map of North America),
    20 (except acorns)

Crabtree Publishing Company

www.crabtreebooks.com   1-800-387-7650

Printed in China/042011/CP20110131

Cataloging-in-Publication Data
Aloian, Molly.
  Life of the California coast nations / Molly Aloian & Bobbie Kalman.
      p. cm. -- (Native nations of North America series)
  Includes index.
  ISBN 0-7787-0382-7 (RLB) -- ISBN 0-7787-0474-2 (pbk.)
  1. Indians of North America--California--History. 2. Indians of North America--California--Social life and customs. I. Kalman, Bobbie. II. Title. III. Native nations of North America.
  E78.C2A46 2005
  979.4004'970146--dc22
                                    2004011118
                                           LC

**Published in
the United States**
PMB 59051
350 Fifth Ave.
59th Floor
New York, NY
10118

**Published
in Canada**
616 Welland Ave.,
St. Catharines, Ontario
Canada
L2M 5V6

**Published in the
United Kingdom**
Maritime House
Basin Road North, Hove
BN41 1WR

**Published
in Australia**
386 Mt. Alexander Rd.,
Ascot Vale (Melbourne)
VIC 3032

Contents

The coast of California

Indigenous, or Native, people have lived along the coast of present-day California for at least 10,000 years. Native groups with traditional **territories** on the coast—and on the islands nearby—include the Chumash, the Coast Miwok, the Gabrielino/Tongva, the Ohlone (Costanoan), the Payomkawichum-Acjachemem (Luiseño-Juaneño), the Pomo, and the Salinan people. The map below shows the traditional territories of these groups. This book describes the lives of these people as they lived before European explorers arrived to settle in California in the 1700s.

N

Pomo

Coast Miwok

Ohlone

PACIFIC OCEAN

Salinan

Chumash

Gabrielino/ Tongva

Chumash

Gabrielino/ Tongva

Payomkawichum-Acjachemem

*The ocean and the **inland** forested areas provided the native people with plenty of food and **natural resources**, or useful materials available in nature.*

The coastal area
The coast stretches about 1,100 miles (1770 km) along the Pacific Ocean from the present-day city of Oregon to the present-day country of Mexico. The coast is made up of three major regions—the northern region, the central region, and the southern region. The **climate** along the coast is mild and wet, but the southern coastal region is generally warmer and drier than the central and northern regions are.

4

Spanish names

Long before European explorers arrived in California, the Native people along the coast lived in thousands of separate groups called **bands**. Most bands contained between 50 and 500 people. Some had up to 2,000 people. Each band had its own language, customs, and traditions. Each also had its own Native name and its own territory. When Spanish explorers and Roman Catholic **missionaries**, or priests, arrived to settle in California during the 1700s, they organized several bands into larger groups, known today as **nations**, and gave them different names. For example, they re-named all the Ohlone bands "costeños" (Costanoan), which means "coast people" in Spanish. Other bands were named after Spanish **missions** that were built on or near Native territories. The name "Gabrielino" refers to a Spanish mission called "San Gabriel," which was built on the territories of the Tongva people. Although some Native names have been forgotten or lost over time, many of today's California nations are using their traditional names once again.

The painting above shows a Chumash family. Along the coast, there are steep cliffs, beaches, flat lands, and hilly areas. This family's home is built high above a beach.

Village groups

Each band of people lived in a **village group**. A village group was made up of one or more large, main villages surrounded by a cluster of small villages. Although the people of most village groups had similar ways of life, there were still important differences among them. For example, the bands that lived in the southern region had different customs than the bands that lived in the northern region had. Once a band formed a village within its territory, the band rarely changed its location.

Separate territories

Some bands lived along the coast, whereas others lived farther inland. Most bands had both coastal and inland territories, however. Territories were large and included specific fishing, hunting, and gathering spots. Territorial boundaries were respected by all the bands. People were careful not to trespass on one another's territories. Some bands, however, granted their neighbors permission to hunt animals or gather foods and materials from their territories.

Different languages

In most cases, the people of each band spoke different languages. Each language belonged to a distinct **language family**, or a group of languages with similar origins or features. The Pomo, the Salinan, and the Chumash people spoke languages that belonged to the Hokan language family. The Gabrielino/Tongva and Payomkawichum-Acjachemem languages belonged to the Uto-Aztecan language family. The Coast Miwok and the Ohlone people spoke languages that were part of the Penutian language family.

Different dialects

The people of some bands—especially those who lived in neighboring territories—spoke the same language, but they often spoke their own **dialects**, or versions of the language. For example, all Gabrielino/Tongva people spoke the same language, known today simply as Gabrielino. The Gabrielino/Tongva bands who lived in the present-day Los Angeles basin, however, spoke different dialects of this language than the dialects spoken by the bands living just outside the Los Angeles basin.

Temporary camps

At certain times of the year, some members of each band left their villages and traveled to different parts of their territories to find food and natural resources. They set up temporary camps near their traditional hunting, fishing, or gathering spots. People from inland bands often camped in their coastal territories when it was time to gather foods such as clams, crabs, and oysters from the ocean. Coastal bands set up camps in their inland territories when it was time to hunt deer or gather materials for shelters.

People were able to set up and take down their temporary camps in about a day.

Clans, moieties, and chiefs

A band was made up of one or more families that included parents and their children, as well as **extended families**. Extended families are groups of relations including aunts, uncles, cousins, and grandparents. These families lived and worked together in their village groups. The people of some bands were also organized into larger groups called **clans** and **moieties**.

Clans

Ohlone, Payomkawichum-Acjachemem, and Salinan people were members of clans. Clans were related family groups that were made up of people who shared the same **ancestors**. Most clans were **patrilineal**.

Patrilineal means that children became parts of their fathers' clans as soon as they were born. When an Ohlone, Payomkawichum-Acjachemem, or Salinan woman got married, she often went to live with her husband and his clan, in or near his father's home.

Moieties

Some bands were also organized into larger groups called moieties. The word "moiety" comes from a French word meaning "one half." Moieties divided people into two groups, regardless of their family ties. For example, Ohlone people belonged to one of two moieties—the Bear moiety or the Deer moiety.

Village leaders

Depending on its size, each village group had one or more **chiefs**, or leaders. Chiefs were responsible for making decisions for the entire village. Most chiefs were men, but some villages had female chiefs. Many chiefs led entire villages, but some chiefs ruled only over clans within their villages. All the people in a village had to approve of a person before he or she was chosen to be become the village chief.

A chief's responsibilities

The chief was an important member of the village and often had several responsibilities, including meeting and welcoming visitors, overseeing hunting and gathering activities, and organizing and leading ceremonies. The chief offered advice to individuals and settled disputes between people or among villages. He or she was also a leader during times of conflict or war.

Ranking people

Pomo and Gabrielino/Tongva bands **ranked**, or gave special positions to, certain members of their bands. Wealthy village members were often ranked very highly. The rankings of people were based on their family backgrounds or on their personal achievements.

*Wealthy and respected village members usually became chiefs. Older male chiefs often passed their positions on to their sons. If a chief did not have a son, the position was passed on to the chief's sister or daughter. A male chief was sometimes known as the **head man** and a female chief as the **head woman**.*

9

Family life

Family members worked hard to make sure that their entire family had enough food and supplies. The men and boys hunted and fished, whereas the women and girls made clothing and baskets or gathered and prepared foods for the other family members. Everyone pitched in to help with big tasks such as gathering materials, building shelters, and collecting acorns.

The lives of children

The birth of a baby was a special occasion. Babies and children were cared for by their parents and extended families. As soon as they were old enough, children were taught how to help their parents with daily chores and tasks. Young boys often learned how to hunt and fish by watching and helping their fathers. Girls learned how to prepare food and make baskets and other household items by assisting their mothers. Older children also helped care for their younger siblings.

Respect for elders

All children were taught to respect their parents and the **elders**. Elders were old or wise members of bands. Young boys and girls were encouraged to listen and be polite to elders. In return, elders told stories and showed the children how to participate in special ceremonies.

Marriage

When they were old enough, boys and girls were expected to marry and start their own families. Parents often chose marriage partners for their children. Some people were allowed to select their own husbands and wives, but they never married against the wishes of their families.

Creating alliances

Some male band members, including **ceremonial leaders** and chiefs, had more than one wife. Marriage was one way that two families formed an **alliance**, or a friendly association. An alliance often resulted in two families joining their territories. Once their territories were joined, more foods and materials were available to the members of both families. Many bands did not have formal marriage ceremonies, but some had feasts and exchanged gifts to celebrate a new marriage. The groom and his family usually gave a gift to the bride and her family.

Materials from nature

obsidian knifeblades

wooden throwing stick

stone mortars and pestles for grinding foods

willowbark skirt

Natural resources were abundant along the coast and in the inland forested areas. These resources were important to the Native people, who used them in order to survive. People gathered natural materials to make various types of shelters, canoes and rafts, cooking utensils, hunting and fishing tools, weapons, and woven items such as baskets.

Using every part

When people hunted animals for food, they used every part of the animals. The skins and furs were fashioned into clothing and blankets, which were worn during the chilly winter months. Bones and antlers were used to make spoons and cooking utensils. Feathers were often used as decorations on clothing or baskets.

Trees, grasses, and more

Trees were valued for their wood and bark. Shelters and canoes were made of wood, as were weapons such as harpoons, bows, and arrows. Bark was also woven into clothing, such as a woman's apron or skirt or a man's **breechcloth**. People also wove grasses to make shelters, canoes, baskets, and clothing such as grass skirts. Soapstone, sandstone, animal bones, and shells were used to fashion a variety of tools, including bowls, fish hooks, and the **mortars and pestles** shown on this page. Many people made sharp knifeblades and arrowheads from **obsidian**.

12

Shell money

There were plenty of shellfish such as clams, mussels, dentaliums, olivella, and abalone along the Pacific coast. People collected and ate these foods and saved the shells. The shells were made into **currency**, or money. First, pieces of the shells were shaped, drilled, and polished. The shells were then fastened together on a thin string of plant fiber or animal skin. The color and thickness of the shells often determined their value. Value also depended on the number of shells and the length of the strings. People used the shells as money for trading. Items such as meat and obsidian could be purchased with strings of these disk-shaped shells. People also used the shells in gambling games. See page 24 for more about trade among bands.

Fish hooks, earrings, and necklaces, including the Pomo necklace above, were also made from various types of shells.

Controlled fires

Inland forested areas provided Native people with many important plants and animals. Native people respected the land and knew how to keep it healthy. They knew that dead or dried-out plants caught fire easily and that **wildfires** were hard to put out. To prevent wildfires, the people of some bands set plants on fire to get rid of the dry, dangerous materials. They made sure the fires burned only in certain areas. Burning old dried-out plants and grasses made more room for healthy new plants to grow. Young plants produced more seeds, nuts, and fruits. The young sprouts attracted more grazing animals, including deer, elk, and antelope. People could then hunt these grazing animals for their meat, skins, and furs.

Shelters

People made various types of shelters using natural materials such as wood, bark, grass, and earth. They built family homes, as well as shelters for ceremonies, dances, and special meetings. Homes were usually built in small groups. Certain shelters, including some ceremonial **sweatlodges**, were **semi-subterranean**, or partly underground.

Family homes

Most of the homes built along the coast were cone-shaped with rounded roofs. People used wooden poles to make the frames for their homes. The poles were either leaned together or pounded into the ground and arched toward the center, where they were tied together with plant fibers. The wooden frames were then covered with reeds, **tule**, brush, grass, bark, or driftwood. A fire in the center of the home gave off light and heat. A hole in the roof let in sunlight and let out smoke. Homes usually held six or seven people, but large homes were sometimes built to hold 50 or more people. Some family homes were semi-subterranean, like the sweatlodges.

Members of an Ohlone family gather to eat in front of their home.

14

ramada

Ramadas

Some bands constructed rectangular shelters called **ramadas** near their homes. A ramada, shown above, had open sides and a flat roof made of wooden poles that were covered with brush or grass. During the summer months, ramadas provided shelter from the hot sun and shaded people who were weaving baskets or doing other chores. The people in some villages also used their ramadas for special ceremonies.

Sweatlodges

The people of most villages had one or more round earth-covered sweatlodges built near their homes. Many sweatlodges were semi-subterranean. They were usually built four to five feet (1.2-1.5 m) into the ground or were dug into the side of a creek or a stream. Small sweatlodges were often used as meeting places for the men in a village to come together to talk and pray. Large sweatlodges were sometimes used for ceremonies.

sweatlodge

Other structures

People also built **storehouses** and other structures out of short branches or out of brush and grass bundles, shown right. Storehouses were used to protect foods from rain or from being eaten by animals. Other structures included singing houses for singing and dance houses for dancing. Some ceremonial structures had low walls and were built without roofs.

Moving on water

Native people often traveled from place to place on **waterways**, such as lakes, rivers, streams, and ocean waters, near their territories. Coastal bands traveled and fished in the Pacific Ocean. Inland territories contained rivers, lakes, and streams. These waterways flowed into one another and eventually emptied into the Pacific Ocean. People used the waterways to travel to hunting, fishing, and gathering areas or to spots where they could collect driftwood, bark, and other natural materials. They also used the waterways to travel to other villages, where they traded or purchased goods that were not available in their territories. People used canoes, and tule, log, or driftwood rafts to travel on the waterways.

Tomols

Chumash and Gabrielino/Tongva people fashioned swift lightweight canoes, called *tomols* or *ti'ats*, from redwood or pine **planks**. They tied the planks together with plant fibers and sealed any holes with a thick, waterproof substance called **asphaltum**, which was found in Chumash and Gabrielino/Tongva territories. Tomols were 12 to 30 feet (3.7-9.1 m) long and held up to ten people. People used double-ended paddles to propel the canoes through water. Some canoes were even sturdy enough to travel on rough ocean waters.

Rafts

Some people used rafts called **balsas** to travel over calm or shallow waterways. Balsas were made from long stalks of tule bundled tightly together with plant fibers. Tule stalks were lightweight and **buoyant**, or able to float. If a balsa became **waterlogged**, or soaked with water, it was left in the sun to dry out. When it was dry, the balsa could be used again. Rafts were also made from logs and driftwood, which were tied together with plant fibers. Long poles or double-edged paddles were used to steer rafts through shallow waters.

log raft

balsa

Food from the land and water

During certain times of the year, people in a village traveled to specific hunting, fishing, and gathering spots within their territories. They returned to these areas year after year. Temporary camps were often set up while the work was being done. Most people worked together in groups, but some hunters preferred to work on their own.

Hunting

Native people knew where to find animals that would provide their families with meat and other important materials. In summer, coastal bands often traveled to their inland territories to hunt a variety of animals, including elk, deer, antelope, rabbits, raccoons, and squirrels. Groups of Chumash, Ohlone, and Gabrielino/Tongva men often hunted rabbits. Inland bands also traveled to the coast to hunt sea otters, sea lions, and other sea mammals. In order to ensure good luck, some hunters did not eat or ate only certain foods for a few days before a hunt.

Fishing

Fishers knew the best fishing locations and returned to them every year. Many people caught salmon, sturgeon, and trout from rivers, streams, and creeks. Some fished from canoes and rafts, using harpoons. Others caught fish with hooks and lines, nets, traps, or spears. The people of some bands used another fishing method. They placed plants that were poisonous to fish in shallow pools of still water. After the fish died, they were collected and eaten.

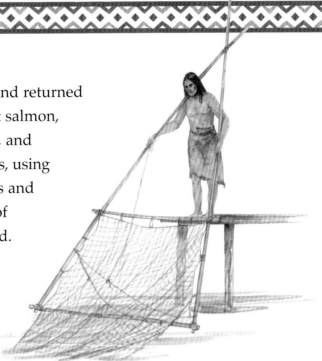

*Fishers used large, long-handled nets called **dip nets** to catch fish and other foods from lakes, rivers, and streams.*

Gathering

People also knew where to collect the plants they needed for food and where to find the materials they needed to build shelters, canoes, and rafts. They gathered acorns, berries, seeds, bulbs, and roots, as well as driftwood, bark, grasses, and plant fibers. Inland bands traveled to the coast to gather clams, mussels, crabs, and oysters. Some foods, including acorns, seaweed, and kelp, were stored and saved for winter, when fewer fresh foods were available. Acorns were stored in **granaries**, or large containers used for storing grains and nuts.

Women used long, pointed sticks to dig up roots and bulbs from the soil.

19

Harvesting acorns

Acorns are the nuts that grow on oak trees. Harvesting acorns was a time-consuming task that often involved an entire village. Acorns were a **staple** food for many bands living in the region. They were specially prepared before they were eaten.

All acorns contain **tannic acid**, which makes them extremely bitter. Women **leached**, or removed, the tannic acid from the acorns to make them **edible**, or fit to eat. Once the acorns were leached, they were made into various foods, including breads, cakes, and soups.

Setting up camp

In autumn, people organized special trips for collecting acorns. They traveled to oak **groves**, or areas where many oak trees grew in one place, and camped nearby for two to three weeks. Certain species of oak trees, such as the tan oak and black oak, produced acorns that were preferred over others. Some people traveled long distances to reach groves of these trees. Harvesting acorns was a special activity, but it was done only once a year. Many bands performed ceremonies and rituals to celebrate harvest time.

Collecting and drying

Elderly village members, women, and children gathered acorns from the ground and placed them in large baskets. Young men and boys used long wooden sticks to knock down any acorns left in the trees. Boys sometimes climbed up the trees to shake out the acorns. People made sure they gathered acorns from different groves because they believed that trees that were not harvested would not produce acorns in the years to come. After collecting large amounts of nuts, the people removed the shells and left the acorns in the sun to dry. Dried acorns were stored for up to a year.

Grinding and leaching

Heavy stones were used to grind the dried acorns into fine **meal**, or flourlike granules. When the acorn meal was fine enough, the bitter-tasting tannic acid was leached from it. Leaching involved two main steps. First, the meal was spread out in a shallow hole in the sand or in the ground, which was lined with leaves or grass. Several containers of water were then poured onto the meal. As the water seeped through the meal, it washed the tannic acid into the sand or ground below. The leached meal could then be baked or boiled in water and mixed with meat, greens, or dried fish.

Beautiful everyday items

Native people made all the items they needed from natural materials. They gathered grasses, roots, and plant fibers to make various types of baskets. They collected bone, shells, stone, and other materials to make jewelry, tools, and musical instruments. These items were both beautiful and functional.

Beautiful baskets

Many California bands, including those that lived along the coast, were well known for their baskets. They wove baskets of all shapes and sizes. Making baskets was usually a woman's job, but some men helped make baskets for their households. Basket makers carefully and quickly wove the fibers together and often decorated them with shells or beads. Some Pomo basket makers made feathered baskets by weaving woodpecker feathers into the stitching. These baskets were often decorated with abalone shells and clamshell disk beads.

Different functions

The style of a basket depended on its function. Different baskets were made for preparing and cooking foods, storing items, and transporting goods. Some baskets were woven tightly enough to hold water! Many women used their basket-making skills to fashion other woven items such as mats, caps, bird traps, and trays.

Some baskets were made to be traded or given as gifts.

A seed beater was used to knock grass seeds off bushes.

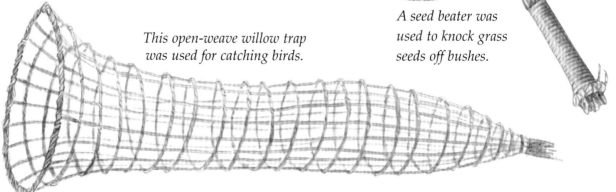

This open-weave willow trap was used for catching birds.

Soapstone objects

Coastal people made bowls, pipes, cooking utensils, and animal carvings from a type of soft soapstone called **steatite**. Steatite can be easily shaped, carved, and polished. Chumash and Gabrielino/Tongva people carved many soapstone objects, including miniature boats that were believed to bring good luck to fishers on fishing trips. They also carved small models of animals such as birds, whales, and seals.

steatite pelican

steatite whale

clapper stick

rattle

Musical instruments

Music was an important part of many dances and ceremonies. People created musical instruments, including whistles, flutes, **clapper sticks**, and rattles, out of natural materials such as wood, shells, animal hides, and bones. Flutes and whistles were made of wood or bone. To make sounds, people blew across the ends of the whistles and blew into the flutes. Rattles were made from large cocoons, shells, or bunches of deer hooves. Rattles and clapper sticks were struck against the palm of the hand to make a sound. They were used to start and keep a beat. Some people made drums by stretching deer hides over wooden frames.

Trading goods

Trade was an important part of life in many villages. Trading allowed people to acquire goods, foods, and resources that were not available near their villages. People exchanged goods or purchased them with shell money. Most trading took place among village groups that lived in neighboring territories. Some people went on trade expeditions to villages that were farther away, however. The people of some bands held special trade feasts at certain times of the year.

Certain territories had resources that were not available in all areas. For example, steatite was an important resource found in Gabrielino/Tongva territory. The Gabrielino/Tongva bands offered steatite to other bands, including the Chumash and the Payomkawichum-Acjachemem. People also traded shells, obsidian, plants that were used for medicines, and foods including salt, nuts, herbs, seeds, and dried fish. Pomo women made baskets that were so admired by other bands, that they were offered for trade.

Pomo trade feasts

Some Pomo bands traded goods or foods with the people of other villages at trade feasts. If a Pomo band had more fish than its members needed, the band held a feast and invited the people from surrounding villages to attend. The visitors brought strings of shell money to the feast. After several days of feasting, the Pomo people determined how much fish they could exchange for the visitors' shell money. Hosting trade feasts allowed the Pomo to trade foods that were plentiful in exchange for money or goods that they needed or wanted. Trade feasts also gave young Pomo men and women an opportunity to meet possible marriage partners from neighboring villages.

shell money

fish

Trading throughout California

The Chumash, Coast Miwok, Gabrielino/Tongva, Payomkawichum-Acjachemem, Pomo, and Salinan people also traded with people who lived farther inland. The coastal bands supplied inland nations with shell money, beads, sea-otter pelts, steatite, baskets, and furs. Some items, including shell money and beads, were then traded by the inland nations to people who lived as far east as present-day Utah and Arizona. The people of these nations used the shells to decorate clothing and other items. At certain times of the year, coastal traders also traveled inland to trading spots, where they met and exchanged goods with traders from different nations on a regular basis.

Many changes

In 1542, some coastal Chumash bands encountered Spanish explorers who had started using the Santa Barbara Channel for their long voyages. By the late 1700s, the Europeans had come into contact with Coast Miwok, Chumash, Gabrielino/Tongva, Payomkawichum-Acjachemem, Pomo, and Salinan bands.

Contact with Europeans completely changed the lives of the Native people. Before long, the Spanish claimed ownership of many Native territories. They demanded that the Native people give up their traditional ways of life and work under the rule of the Spanish explorers and Roman Catholic missionaries.

Spanish missionaries did not recognize the spiritual beliefs of the Native people and forced them to practice the Roman Catholic religion. The missionaries also saw no value in traditional Native lifeways.

Devastating diseases

The Spanish explorers, soldiers, and missionaries who entered the central and southern coastal regions carried infectious diseases, such as smallpox, influenza, and cholera. Native people had never before come into contact with these diseases and many became ill soon after meeting Europeans or handling European goods. The diseases spread quickly through many Native village groups. Entire families and bands died as a result.

(above) Europeans brought goods from Europe that the Native people had never before seen or used, including alcohol, metal knifeblades, and cloth. Native people began wearing European clothing and traded cloth with one another.

Other changes

As the Spanish claimed Native lands for themselves, they began building missions on territories where Native people had once hunted, fished, and gathered. As more European settlers arrived in the region, they brought new and different plants to North America. Over time, the crops, grasses, and weeds the Europeans planted in Native territories took over the seed grasses on which the Native people had relied for food. As more and more Europeans settled in Native territories, the amounts of available wild game and ocean foods also started to decrease. Europeans took more animals than they needed for survival. They began **overhunting** the animals, leaving the Native people fewer deer, elk, and antelope to hunt.

The missions

In the mid 1700s, missionaries began building Roman Catholic churches on the southern and central coastal regions. The first mission was set up in 1769 by Gaspar de Portolà and a priest named Junípero Serra in present-day San Diego. During the following years, twenty-one other missions were created on Native territories between the present-day cities of San Diego and San Francisco. Thousands of Native people were forced to move from their villages and live and work at the missions. Missionaries tried to **convert** the Native people, or convince them to change their religious beliefs. They were determined to teach the Native people European ways of life, which included farming and carpentry. Some Native people moved into the missions in order to survive, but many did not want to give up their spiritual beliefs and traditional ways of life. Those who refused to change their ways were often severely punished.

The missionaries banned Native ceremonies and dancing. Some Native groups, including the Ohlone shown above, continued to practice their ceremonies regardless of the bans. Others combined their ceremonies with Christian beliefs.

Changed ways of life

Life at the missions was very difficult for the Native people. They were forced to wear European clothing, speak Spanish, and practice Christianity. They were also forced to work extremely hard as farmers, carpenters, and blacksmiths. European diseases spread quickly throughout the missions, and many Native people died as a result. Some refused to be mistreated or give up their traditional ways of life. These people escaped from the missions and moved farther inland. Others rebelled against the missionaries in an attempt to return to their traditional ways of life.

Mexican control

In 1833, the Mexican government took control of several Spanish missions. It promised the Native people that the mission lands would be divided equally between the government and the Native people. The government did not keep its promise to share the lands, however. It kept much of the land and then built large ranches. Many Native people were forced to live and work on these ranches.

Reservations

The United States government took possession of California in 1848. Many bands were forced to live on **reservations**, or small areas of land that were set aside for Native people by the government, during the 1850s. While living on the reservations, many Native people felt pressure to give up their languages and cultures.

This cross marks the graves of several Native people who worked at the San Diego mission.

Non-Native relatives
During the years when Mexican and Spanish governments controlled California, many Native men and women married Spanish and Mexican men and women. The children from these marriages eventually married non-Native people as well. Today, Native people in California have both Native and non-Native relatives.

The nations today

Today, thousands of Coast Miwok, Chumash, Gabrielino/Tongva, Payomkawichum-Acjachemem, Ohlone, Pomo, and Salinan people live in California and in other areas throughout the United States. Many bands work hard to preserve their arts, languages, cultures, traditions, and sacred places. Native people continue to participate in traditional song and dance. They also make crafts such as baskets in the traditional ways, and they eat traditional foods, including acorn soup. Other Native people run successful **casinos**, or places where people gamble money. **Descendants** of some bands continue to live together on their reservations. They are proud of their cultures and languages and value their heritages. Many people are also relearning the traditional languages and teaching them to their children.

The picture above is called Chumash Ways. *It was painted by Mitchell E. Robles, a contemporary Chumash artist.*

Federal recognition

Today, there are more Native Americans living in California than in any other state. Several California bands are currently seeking **federal recognition** by the United States government. Federal recognition allows a band to have status as a nation in the eyes of the United States government. When a band becomes recognized, its members are able to represent their own rights and interests. The people are then able to protect and preserve their rights and interests for many years to come.

Several of today's Pomo basket makers are well known for their beautiful and intricate baskets. This small basket is being woven in the traditional Pomo way.

Glossary

Note: Boldfaced terms that are defined in the text may not appear in the glossary.

ancestor A person from whom another person is descended

band A group of people—often relatives—who speak a similar language, have similar customs and traditions, and who live together in one or more villages

breechcloth A long piece of soft leather worn by men and boys that was gathered between the legs and pulled over a belt

ceremonial leader A person who acts as a leader during special ceremonies

climate The long-term weather conditions in an area, including temperature, rainfall, and wind

descendant A person who comes from a particular ancestor or group of ancestors

inland Describing an area or region that is not near the ocean

mission A village where Roman Catholic missionaries taught Native people about Christianity and European ways of life

mortar and pestle A bowl and a hand-held tool used to grind or mash foods

nation A group of Native people with a common language, culture, and history

obsidian A type of glass that is very hard and usually black in color

overhunt To hunt more animals than are needed for survival

plank A thin, flat wooden board used for constructing canoes

staple An important food that is used daily

territory An area of land and water on which a group of people traditionally lived, hunted, fished, and gathered food

tule A type of plant that grows near water

waterway A body of water, such as a lake

wildfire A raging fire in nature that spreads quickly and is difficult to put out

Index